Europe

Pentothal Postcards

by David C. Lai MD

Mark Batty Publisher

First Edition

10 9 8 7 6 5 4 3 2 1

Copyright © 2005 Dr. David C. Lai
The design of this edition © 2005 Steve Byers

This edition ©2005
Mark Batty Publisher, LLC
6050 Boulevard East, Suite 2H
West New York, New Jersey 07093
www.markbattypublisher.com

Library of Congress Cataloging-in-Publication data:

Lai, David, MD
Pentathol postcards / By David Lai, MD – 1st ed.
p. cm.
Includes index
ISBN 0-9725636-6-0 (alk paper)
1. Advertising postcards– Catalogs. 2. Advertising– Drugs– Pictorial works. 3. Abbott laboratories– Collectibles– Catalogs. I. Title

HF6146.P6L34 2005

659.19'6157822 – dc22

Printed and bound at the National Press
The Hashemite Kingdom of Jordan

Acknowledgements

I thank Rick Steinbrook, Carol Warfield, Charlie McLeskey, Adrian Padfield, Will Hughes and Dan Whalen for their support and encouragement. A.J. Wright is a bibliographic sleuth. Helpful members of the "Dear Doctor" Postcard Collector Page (www. geocities.com/deardr.pc) include: Tom Fortunato, Dan Friedman, Martin Walker, Bill Holland, Henry Ratz, and Tom Breske. Leigh Mercer's Panama palindrome from the November 13, 1948 issue of Notes & Queries courtesy of the Oxford University Press. Steve Shaiman introduced me to Steve Byers. Rolando Castillo and Roberto Gómez Torres clarified the UNAM cards. Finally, I thank my wife Marianne for her continued support and inspiration.

Book design: Steve Byers.
This book is typeset in Linotype's Avenir™ Typeface.

Pentothal Postcards

by David C. Lai MD

An Introduction—
Collecting Pentothal postcards

The Pentothal postcard promotional program is a powerful example of 1950s marketing genius. Between 1954 and 1968, about 170 different cards promoting the Sodium Pentothal anesthetic product shipped from 70 countries, all with local stamping, franking, or both, each featuring in some way the flavor of the moment when they were sent, and the culture of the country from which they came. Collecting Pentothal postcards (with all their variants), is ephemeral urban archeology at its best—no wonder there are a growing number of people who are fascinated by this subject.

Pentothal postcards are an ideal collectible; both sides of each postcard are attractive to look at, often they contain great looking stamps and cancellations, they are high concept, a piece of history, and they have international appeal. What's more, there are all sorts of interesting variants – different languages, stamps, and countries of destination. And, at least at the time of this writing, they are still relatively inexpensive.

If you go to a fair or market where old postcards are sold and look for Pentothal postcards, it is likely you will be disappointed. The subjects that link these cards, Abbott and Sodium Pentothal, are uncommon collecting categories. A recent search of such markets in Chicago turned up a couple of postcards containing an image of Abbott buildings, but they were not part of the Pentothal program, nor had they been sent through the mail, and North Chicago is the home of Abbott Laboratories.

Very often Pentothal postcards were collected by the original recipients – a testament to the perception by the doctors who received them of their intrinsic value – and are now starting to appear on the market some 40 years later. With the advent of the Internet marketplace, the market for ephemeral collectibles is now global. Sometimes it is not even clear from where the acquired postcards will be delivered. We have seen Pentothal postcards coming from a doctor's collection in Buenos Aires in Argentina, from another in Detroit in the USA, and from many other locations.

In the category of medical postcard collectibles, Pentothal postcards seem to be the most prominent, although Abbott was not alone in implementing this idea back in the 1950s. Cards were made with good effect, and using broadly the same concept, for Marezine, the motion travel sickness drug; for Sudafed, the allergy treatment; for Festal, for digestive discomfort; and Merck Sharp & Dohme's mumps shots to name a few. Not all the programs were carried out in exactly the same way: for example, some did not use local stamps, which severely limits their collectible appeal.

In developing this book we have been collecting examples of original cards to use as illustrations. In addition we have been collecting cards to offer as part of a special collector's edition of this book, each of which will include a small number of genuine Pentothal postcards. In days gone by we would have had to sift through trays of cards in many places and it would have taken a lot of time to find enough for our purpose, if indeed we ever succeeded. But now there is the Internet. All of a sudden, rare and buried ephemeral treasures are much more accessible.

Potentially, Pentothal postcards could be collected by people who are interested in the original Abbott program, by stamp collectors, and collectors of cards from a certain time period or place. These categories of collector still amount to a relatively small and specialist market. But there is a steady demand for cards and when one is offered it rarely goes unsold. Our recent investigation has shown that the most popular categories of Pentothal postcard are those containing images of people, the wackier the image the better; those containing images that do a good job of dating the cards such as views that contain old trucks or cars; and those that contain some feature that emphasizes the zeitgeist of the moment, such as grainy or overly brash coloration. Of least interest, and therefore value, seem to be the cards that feature straightforward natural scenes of no particular time period.

The correspondence side of Pentothal postcards substantially adds to the overall experience –

highlighting the role of Pentothal in the place depicted in the card. The messages are written in a choice of languages, and a wide variety of script and lettering styles employing different technologies such as typesetting, typewriter and handwriting. Addresses are placed on the card using different typefaces, different technology and often a label. Then there are the stamps and the way they are franked. Sometimes there is no stamp, but the card is franked: was this always the case, or did a stamp get missed and the card get franked anyway? The combination of these features creates a series of clues that, for the extra curious, can lead to fascinating stories. Here is an example in point:

A Pentothal postcard was stamped and mailed on April 9th, 1962 from Lundy, to a doctor in Pennsylvania. The same card, mailed some years later in 1967 is featured on page 99 of this book. (Often the same postcards were sent in different batches, spanning weeks or even months). Lundy is a place without Pentothal, the card tells us. The card also tells us that Lundy Island is a self-governed dominion about 1.6 miles square, situated some 12 miles from England. We know that the postcard was mailed on April 9th, because it bears a franked Lundy-issued stamp with that date. In addition we know from the history books that this stamp was published in 1957. It is the red "Standing Puffin," bearing the value of 1 Puffin. The one-Puffin stamp allowed the postcard to ship from Lundy to the British mainland. A further British stamp of 2 pence, affixed in Lundy with the Puffin stamp, was what was needed to travel the card from the British mainland to Pennsylvania in the USA. The British cancellation on the card tells us that it took one day in transit to Britain before its onward journey to the USA.

A little background to our Lundy story: Martin Harman, a British financier sometimes known as the "King of Lundy", bought the island in 1925. He first issued Puffin stamps in 1929. He chose the Puffin as his standard of value because the islanders in the early part of the nineteenth century did a brisk trade in the feathers of these birds. In 1969, seven years after our postcard was mailed, Jack Haywood, another prosperous businessman, bought Lundy and gave it to the British people. The National Trust now administers the island, which has become a destination for tourists.

With the Lundy example, we have a hint of the many stories behind these cards. How many other amusing and intriguing stories lie behind these cards? We invite you to explore for yourself!

Steve Byers
Huntington, New York

The Pentothal postcard program
The first known mailing of an Abbott Laboratories postcard advertising the anesthetic Pentothal took place in 1954. This book reproduces the most interesting of these "Pentothal Postcards" from Abbott Laboratories—the longest-running advertising campaign of its kind (it ran until 1968) with the most cards mailed. The cards in this book are more than medical junk mail from a bygone era. They are a portal into world exploration. They tell the stories of fascinating people and places, and the creative and successful way a company marketed its product.

History—"Dear Doctor" Postcards
Postcards have long been an inexpensive advertising medium. Drug companies often sent physicians "Dear Doctor" postcards to promote new drugs, recruiting staff from across the globe to send them, so that each bore postmarks from around the world. These colorful "tourist" postcards captured the attention of the receivers with their pictures, and promoted their products through messages on the reverse.

An early example of this type of advertising campaign was launched by the Reinschild Chemical Company from Helfenberg, Germany, in 1914. The postcards from the pharmaceutical company read: "DEAR DOCTOR: In this 'Special Message' we will confide to you the most infallible way to Defer Old Age and Preserve Youth."

The heyday of "Dear Doctor" postcards was from the 1950s to 1960s. During this time, Abbott Laboratories, the pharmaceutical company, launched their postcard advertisements for their familiar intravenous anesthetic. The Abbott campaign is now a slice of advertising history which helped make Sodium Pentothal an important part of medical history.

Context— A Romance with Travel

Interest in world travel was especially keen in 1956 with the release of the highly publicized and well-loved film *Around the World in Eighty Days*, and Abbott took advantage of America's romance with global tourism with its "Dear Doctor" campaign. In 1956, Abbott sent postcards advertising the anesthetic Pentothal from 19 countries; Argentina, Australia, Belgium, Columbia, England, France, Greece, Ireland, Italy, Peru, Portugal, Scotland, South Africa, Spain, Sweden, Switzerland, United States, Uruguay and the Holy See (the Vatican).

A New Campaign

It is unclear why Abbott started sending postcards in addition to its traditional print advertisements. One theory is that Abbott wanted to showcase the ubiquitousness of Pentothal. Another suggestion is that the expiration of patent rights in 1954 combined with competition from other ultra short-acting barbiturates (Parke, Davis & Company's Surital Sodium [thiamylal sodium] and Schering's Neraval Sodium [methitural sodium]) prompted Abbott to look for ways to maintain Pentothal's market share. R. J. Dubourdieu, Abbott's product advertising manager, described the thought process behind the campaign: "If Pentothal is the world's best documented intravenous anesthetic, perhaps we could capture the interest that almost everybody has in world travel to far-away romantic places." During his tenure Dubourdieu wrote the text on the reverse of the postcards, while Abbott advertising executive Tom Bird was responsible for the logistics of the campaign.

Mysterious Origins

Charless Hahn was stamp editor at the *Chicago Sun-Times*. He and his wife owned *All Americas Publishing Service*, which was contracted to handle the Pentothal postcard mailings. In addition, around 1954, Hahn began publishing a Spanish language magazine promoting Abbott products to Latin American doctors at the request of Tom Bird, the Abbott advertising executive. Dean Carson, product manager for Abbott Laboratories, claimed the postcards were his idea, although Hahn may have been involved, having seen the Evipan (hexobarbital) advertising postcards that Bayer sent from Germany to physicians in his hometown of Buenos Aires, Argentina, in the 1930s.

The origins of the campaign remain a mystery; it is not known which of the four men—Dubourdieu, Bird, Hahn or Carson—actually suggested the use of postcards.

Abbott is not the source to end the debate. The pharmaceutical company routinely destroyed old material every few years, and so unfortunately no cards remain in the company's archive. The number of different cards sent out each year, derived from lists that Dubourdieu was able to uncover, is close to the number of cards actually known to exist (see below.) Numerous variations (different salutations, stamps, cancellations, and languages) of the 166 known different faces of the cards afford plenty of collecting opportunities.

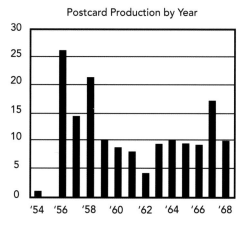

Postcard Production by Year

Just Post It— the Mechanics of the Campaign

Regional Abbott representatives purchased postcards in their territories and arranged for local printing of the advertising message. Most cards were in English; postcards printed in Arabic, Dutch, French, German, Greek, Italian, Portuguese, Spanish and Swedish have also been found. Address labels sent from America were affixed to the cards; sometimes, instead of a label, cards were printed a second time with the destination address. Besides America, cards were sent to Argentina, Australia, Belgium, Canada, Chile, France, Germany, Greece, Hong Kong, Italy, Lebanon, Mexico, Netherlands, Nicaragua, Peru, Portugal, South Africa, Sweden, and Uruguay.

The discovery of "error cards" with mismatched labels or even the wrong message, suggest that some, if not all, of the cards were processed in the United States. Postage stamps were put on the cards, which were then bagged and delivered to the local post office. Many of these cards have had the stamps removed, while others were saved for their interesting postmarks, including first-day of issue cancellations.

Going Postal— Problems along the Way

Abbott's aim to capture unique postmarks from around the world, and the sheer size of the Pentothal postcard project, affected the postal policy of some small territories. The 1961 mailing from Wilkes, Australian

Antarctic Territory, is an example of how the sheer size of the Pentothal postcard project could affect postal policy: out of the 286,000 pieces of mail delivered by the *Magga Dan* ship from Melbourne, Australia to Wilkes, 280,000 pieces were from Abbott. The director of the Antarctic Division complained bitterly about the large quantity of postcards. As a result of this episode, mailing restrictions and alternative postmarking facilities were introduced there.

Other locations also had their share of difficulties. The 1958 mailing from Punta Arenas, Chile, took eight months to complete. It turned out that there was a single part-time postal carrier working one hour a day with a hand cancel stamper.

The postal workers in Copenhagen, Denmark, had to process a mailing a second time after the boat carrying the first shipment sank.

However, the mailing from Baghdad in Iraq proved to be the most frustrating. After stamps were selected and prepaid, printing of the cards could not be completed due to overwhelming bureaucracy and red tape. The postage money was forfeited, and the ancient Ottoman city on the Tigris River was dropped from the schedule.

Other locations on Abbott's list that were scrapped due to various difficulties include Egypt, Malaysia, Kenya, Timbuktu, and Casablanca. Cards from far flung places such as Kuala Lumpur and Nairobi have been found. Other discoveries of cards—and mysteries— remain very possible.

The shortage of trained anesthesiologists during World War II was mirrored in civilian life in America. In 1955, the AANA had 6,340 active members while the ASA had 3,000. This meant that anesthesiologists and CRNA's accounted for less than 5 percent of the 200,000 to 300,000 postcards per mailing. The remaining cards went to non-anesthesiologist physicians as well as pharmacists, hospitals, prisons, and lay people.

Anesthetics and Pentothal— some Background

The Beginning— a Medical Godsend

In the early twentieth century there were very few professional anesthesiologists. Surgeons often utilized "Novocain," local anesthesia, or performed their own spinal anesthesia—and then did the surgery. When general anesthesia was needed, an intern was called upon to "pour a little ether." It was also not uncommon for lay people to give anesthesia. Stories abound of the anesthetic being given by the janitor, the housekeeper, or whoever happened to be walking by.

Ether was the most commonly used anesthetic as it was the safest in random, untrained hands. Inductions were often an interminable, drawn-out struggle for both the patient and the anesthetist: thirty minutes was not uncommon. Patients often had nightmares of the mask going over their face long after the operation was finished. One of the first anesthesiologists to test Pentothal, John Lundy, when confronted with an ether-soaked cloth over his face prior to having his tonsils removed at age twelve, threatened to jump out the window unless the anesthetic could proceed on his terms. For patients (and anesthetists) unable to tolerate ether induction, intravenous induction with Pentothal was a godsend.

Getting Pentothal onto the Medical Scene

Pentothal was introduced in the United States in 1936, with production at Abbott's North Chicago plant, and then, from the following year in Perivale, West London, England.

The introductory process began on April 16, 1934, when Ernest Volwiler and Donalee Tabern of Abbott Laboratories submitted an application to the U.S. Patent Office for "thiobarbituric acid derivatives." Having previously introduced Nembutal in 1929 (pentobarbital, better known as the sleeping pill that Marilyn Monroe overdosed on), they were now working on a quicker acting sulphur drug. Although the

Pentothal patent was not granted until April 11, 1939, it expired twenty years after the date of filing, in 1954.

The serial number "8064" was used in the patent report in place of its long chemical name. The only difference between this compound and Nembutal was the replacement of oxygen with sulphur, a "thio" substitution. Number 8064 became known as thionembutal and eventually, thiopental (Pentothal).

Early Advertising Campaigns

Abbott began promoting Pentothal in its widely distributed in-house publication *What's New* as well as in leading medical journals such as the *Journal of the American Medical Association* (*JAMA*). Those with formal training in administering anesthesia were specifically targeted by Abbott in journals like *Anesthesiology* (sent to physicians of the American Society of Anesthesiologists) and the *Journal of the American Association of Nurse Anesthetists* (sent to the group's nurses).

Publication in a scientific journal has long been a way to validate a new drug or technique. A 1940 Pentothal advertisement already had 89 complete references to articles and papers in journals. The articles quickly became too numerous to cite in full, and soon only the numbers of articles were reported: 300 in 1942; 400 in 1943; 500 in 1944; and 600 in 1945. A 1946 Pentothal advertisement in Canada proclaimed: "More than 748 published reports by leading surgeons and anesthetists over the entire world provide a wealth of accumulated experience on every phase of intravenous anesthesia with Pentothal Sodium." (The accompanying map showing the geographic distribution of Pentothal use distinguishes between civilian and military reports allocation.) Later ad campaigns continued the theme of worldwide availability in advertisements with alluring alliterations. The "Calling" series (1946 – 1949) included: Paris calling Parkville; Mandalay calling Memphis; Deauville calling Des Moines; Pisa calling Peoria; and Florence calling Flagstaff. The 1950 "From" series included: Alexandria to Altoona; Sydney to San Francisco; Lima, Peru to Lima, Ohio; Bombay to Beaumont; and Amsterdam to Aberdeen. A special two-page color spread depicted the various ways Christmas was celebrated "the world over." The "From" series continued in 1951 and 1952 with: Cadiz to Canton; Barcelona to Bismarck; Guatemala to Green Bay; and Addis Ababa to Allentown. Advertisements in medical journals continued the international theme through 1968, but they were joined by a new medium – the picture postcard.

David C. Lai, MD
Gig Harbor, Washington
August 17, 2004

Postcards

Canada · Mountie · Abbott Canada was established 1931 in Montréal.

14

Dear Doctor:

Here in Quebec, just as wherever modern surgery is practiced, Pentothal Sodium has been the subject of an impressive series of reports in the medical press. World wide, more than 2300 articles have been published on intravenous anesthesia with Pentothal since Abbott introduced the drug in 1934. On this solid clinical background rests a growing appreciation of Pentothal's advantages.

Abbott

PENTOTHAL SODIUM
Trade Mark
(Sterile Thiopental Sodium, Abbott)

A MIKE ROBERTS COLOR PRODUCTION, 1231 BLEURY ST., MONTREAL, CANADA
PHOTO COURTESY OF CANADIAN GOVT. TRAVEL BUREAU AND BYRON HARMON
LITHO'D IN CANADA

NATURAL
Color Card

CANADA 2¢

CYRIL J. CORRIGAN, M.D.
825 NICOLLET AVE.
MINNEAPOLIS 2, MINN.
U. S. A.

Greenland · Native sealers from "Qivitoq" (1958) · Fjeldgængeren was a 1956 Danish film.

Native sealers from Greenland,
picture from the Greenland film "QIVITOQ"
taken by Nordisk Film Ko.

16

Dear Doctor:
In vast and sparsely populated Greenland you'll find PENTOTHAL in use, as it is wherever modern medicine is practiced. There is no safer, more effective and versatile intravenous anesthetic the world over.

Abbott

PENTOTHAL® SODIUM
(Thiopental Sodium for Injection, Abbott)

DR. WILSON M. SHAW,
BEVERLY HOSPITAL
HERRICK & HEATHER STS.,
BEVERLY, MASS., U.S.A.

GODTH
11-3-1959

KONGELIG POST
GRØNLAND 15

Mexico · The Little Bull (1958)

18

Dear Doctor:

One of the reasons doctors in Mexico respect and use PENTOTHAL is the nearly 3000 published world reports available to them for reference. That, and a clinical history of nearly 25 years. Good reasons, too, for your trust.

Abbott

PENTOTHAL® SODIUM
(Thiopental Sodium for Injection, Abbott)

MEXICAN POPULAR ART

"The little bull". Pyrotechnical toy in pasteboard, wood and paper. Mexico, D. F.

DR. GEORGE W. HOOVER,
837 N.E. 20TH AVE.,
FORT LAUDERDALE, FLA.
U.S.A.

CROMODIAPOSITIVA: SONIA ARRIOLA BAYER
MANUEL CASAS, IMPRESOR — MÉXICO

United Nations · Flags on display at U.N. (1964) · Wallace Kirkman Harrison, chief architect.

FLAGS ON DISPLAY AT U.N.
The national flags of member nations are
proudly displayed before United Nations
Headquarters in New York City.

20

Dear Doctor,
    These flags, flying
before United Nations
headquarters, symbolize
scores of nations — where
PENTOTHAL (thiopental,
Abbott) is known. No other
intravenous anesthetic is
as widely used — either
here in the U.S.A., or
around the globe.
                    Abbott

PENTOTHAL® SODIUM (Thiopental Sodium, Abbott)

POST CARD

DR. KENNETH GRAY,
85 KING ST., W.
GANANOQUE, ONT.
CANADA

2 —

United States · Waikiki Beach.

WAIKIKI BEACH

22

Aloha, Doctor...
from the 50th State,
Hawaii. Here living
is informal, relaxed. The
climate, superb. And
in the hospitals, you'll
find a familiar name—
PENTOTHAL. Doctors
here put their trust
in PENTOTHAL because
they know it is the
world's most thoroughly
documented intravenous
anesthetic.

Abbott

PENTOTHAL® SODIUM
(Thiopental Sodium for Injection, Abbott)

HONOLULU, HAWAII

DR. EARL A. THOMPSON,
COACHELLA,
CALIFORNIA
U.S.A.

Jamaica · Doctor's Cave, Montego Bay (1964) · Doctor's Cave Bathing Club started in 1906.

24

Doctors Cave, Montego Bay, Jamaica, The W. I.

AUTHENTIC JAMAICA SCENE

PRINTED MATTER

—————— PENTOTHAL® SODIUM (Thiopental Sodium, Abbott) ——————

PRINTED IN U.S.A.

Dear Doctor:
        Physicians who
visit Jamaica will
recognize many
familiar drugs in
daily medical use.
Prominent among the
anesthetics is
PENTOTHAL (Thiopental,
Abbott) — easy to
administer, with smooth
induction and quick
recovery — and tested
by decades of constant
use throughout the
world.
                Abbott

Cuba · Morro Castle (1954) · *Morro Castle*, an ill-fated luxury liner, was launched in 1930.

EL CASTILLO DEL MORRO Y LA AVENIDA DEL PUERTO
Entrada al Puerto
Habana, Cuba

Dear Doctor,

26

More than 2300 reports in medical journals throughout the world have been published on intravenous anesthesia with Pentothal Sodium. Like their colleagues in other countries, doctors here in Cuba find that such exhaustive references, covering every aspect of anesthesia with Pentothal, mean greater convenience, safety, and effectiveness in the employment of this powerful, short—acting agent.

Abbott

Made in U. S. A.
56505
PENTOTHAL SODIUM
Trade Mark
(Sterile Thiopental Sodium, Abbott)

Genuine Natural Color. Made by Dexter Press, Inc., West Nyack, N. Y.

JOSEPH J. HALLERON, M.D.
STATE DEPT. OF HEALTH,
ALBANY 1, N.Y.
U.S.A.

Barbados · Beach scene at Barbados (1967)
Bearded Fig Trees were once so dense that Portuguese sailors named the island Barbados or 'Bearded One'.

Beach scene at Barbados

Dear Doctor:

Come visit Barbados, here in the beautiful West Indies. The climate's ideal. You'll be welcomed by old friends too. Among them is PENTOTHAL (thiopental) — an intravenous agent of choice here as in lands the world around.

Abbott

BARBADOS 8 cents

PENTOTHAL® SODIUM (Sodium Thiopental, Abbott)

PRINTED IN U.S.A.

U S A

DR ROY E WALLACE
32 CAYUGA ST
SENECA FALLS NY 13148
U S A

PRINTED MATTER

Panama · Miraflores Locks (1957)

ESCLUSAS DE MIRAFLORES
MIRAFLORES LOCKS

30

Distinguido Doctor:

There is no safer, more effective intravenous anesthetic the world over than
Pentothal Sodium. You'll find
it here in Panama, the international crossroads, as you
will wherever modern sur-
gery is practiced.

Abbott

PENTOTHAL® SODIUM
(Sterile Thiopental Sodium, Abbott)

EMERY F. WILL, M.D.
83 MAIN ST.,
BATAVIA, N.Y.
U.S.A.

Mexico · The University City Rectorate (1968) · Allegorical mural by Juan O'Gorman.

32

Rectoría de la C. U. México, D. F. **TARJETA POSTAL**
The University City Rectorate.

PRINTED
MATTER

Ediciones "FEMA", S. A. Apartado 7190 México D. F.

PENTOTHAL® SODIUM (Sodium Thiopental, Abbott)

Dear Nurse Anesthetist:
Greetings from sunny Mexico, where you're sure to find old friends! Important among these is PENTOTHAL (thiopental). This agent of choice is a favorite among anesthetists here, as around the globe.
Abbott

SARAH S PONESMITH
206 BOSLER AV
LEMOYNE PA 17043
U S A

Hecho en México

Mexico · Centro Medico (1963) · Leon Trotsky was killed with an ice-axe in 1940 in Mexico.

CENTRO MEDICO — México, D. F.

34

Dear Doctor:
   Doctors in Mexico City
are proud of this newly
completed Medical Center.
They have spared no
effort to equip it with
the very finest. Their choice
among anesthetics naturally
includes PENTOTHAL
(Thiopental, Abbott). No
other intravenous anesthetic
can offer so long a record
of sureness and relative
safety.
             Abbott

PENTOTHAL® SODIUM (Thiopental Sodium, Abbott)

DE. DEBORAH KATZ,
209 RAGLAN AVE.
TORONTO 10, ONT.
CANADA.

AERIAL PHOTO OF MAIN PLANT AND HOME OFFICES,
ABBOTT LABORATORIES, NORTH CHICAGO, ILLINOIS.

United States · North Chicago, Illinois (1950) · Abbott home office.

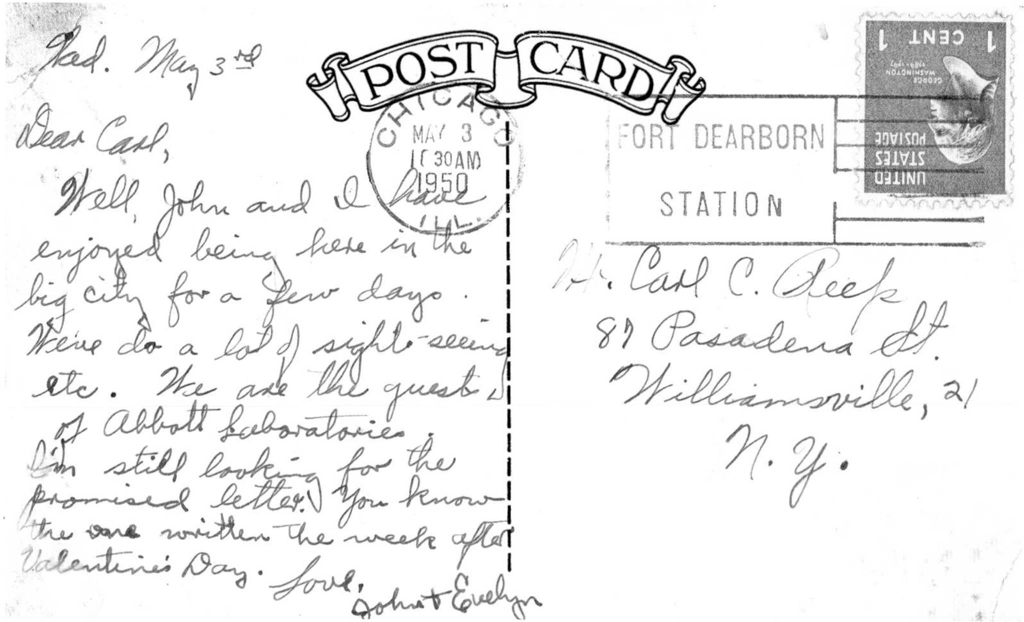

Wed. May 3rd

Dear Carl,

Well, John and I have
enjoyed being here in the
big city for a few days.
We've do a lot of sight-seeing
etc. We are the guests
of Abbott Laboratories.
I'm still looking for the
promised letter. You know
the one written the week after
Valentine's Day. Love,
John & Evelyn

POST CARD

CHICAGO
MAY 3
11 30 AM
1950
ILL.

FORT DEARBORN
STATION

Mr. Carl C. Peek
81 Pasadena St.
Williamsville, 21
N. Y.

36

United States · Lower Manhattan, from Governor's Island (1956) · Originally called Nutten Island for its groves of chestnut trees.

**LOWER MANHATTAN, FROM GOVERNOR'S ISLAND
NEW YORK CITY**

38

Dear Doctor:

Here in New York, as wherever modern surgery is practiced, Pentothal Sodium continues to grow in favor for intravenous anesthesia. A solid background of more than 2300 articles published in the world medical press confirms Pentothal's advantages: quick response, moment to moment control, smooth, painless induction and pleasant, swift recovery.

Abbott

PENTOTHAL SODIUM
Trade Mark
(Sterile Thiopental Sodium, Abbott)

PRINTED IN U.S.A. — CURTEICHCOLOR® REPRODUCTION FROM KODACHROME OR EKTACHROME ORIGINAL

D-11171

BUILD YOUR FUTURE
WISELY, SAFELY
U.S. SAVINGS BONDS

U.S. POSTAGE 2¢

R.
MAN.,

Mexico · The University City (1968) · Rectoria Tower & Central Library of The Universidad Nacional Autónoma de México.

40

Ciudad Universitaria,
México. D. F.
The University City,
México, D. F.

TARJETA POSTAL

PRINTED
MATTER

Ediciones "FEMA", S.A. Apartado 7190 México D.F. ——— PENTOTHAL® SODIUM (Sodium thiopental, Abbott)

Dear Nurse Anesthetist:
Greetings from
sunny Mexico, where
you're sure to find old
friends! Important among
these is PENTOTHAL
(thiopental). This agent
of choice is a favorite
among anesthetists here,
as around the globe.
Abbott

KATHRYN L KELLY
17500 WESTMORELAND RD
DETROIT MICH 48219
U S A

Hecho en México

CORREOS 20¢ MEXICO 68

Mexico · Public works and communications building (1956) · 19 different Pentothal Postcards were sent from Mexico.

42

Dear Doctor:

Here in Mexico, as wherever modern surgery is practiced, Pentothal Sodium continues to grow in favor for intravenous anesthesia. A solid background of more than 2300 articles published in the world medical press confirms Pentothal's advantages: quick response, moment to moment control, smooth, painless induction and pleasant, swift recovery.

Abbott

PENTOTHAL SODIUM
Trade Mark
Sterile Thiopental Sodium, Abbott

PUBLIC WORKS AND COMMUNICATIONS BUILDING, MEXICO, D. F.

Lito en México.

5 CTS CORREOS MEXICO

JOHN A. CRAWFORD, M.D.
23 E. OHI ST.
INDIANAPOLIS 4, IND.
U.S.A.

Mexico · El Castillo y las Mil Columnas, Chichén Itzá (1961) · The Pyramid of Kukulkan has 365 steps and one thousand columns.

El Castillo y las Mil Columnas, Chichén Itzá.
Mérida, Yucatán, México

44

Here in the land of Mayas, archeology goes back to pre-Columbian days. But medicine is up to the moment... and PENTOTHAL an anesthetic of choice. Smooth induction, moment-to-moment control, swift recovery. You'll like it too!

Abbott

PENTOTHAL® (Thiopental, Abbott)

C

MRS. SARAH S. PONESMITH
206 BOSLER AVE.
LEMOYNE, PA.
U. S. A.

Mexico · College of Medicine, University City (1956)

46

Dear Doctor:

Here in Mexico, as wherever modern surgery is practiced, Pentothal Sodium continues to grow in favor for intravenous anesthesia. A solid background of more than 2300 articles published in the world medical press confirms Pentothal's advantages: quick response, moment to moment control, smooth, painless induction and pleasant, swift recovery.

Abbott

PENTOTHAL SODIUM
Trade Mark
(Sterile Thiopental Sodium, Abbott)

COLLEGE OF MEDICINE, UNIVERSITY CITY, MEXICO, D. F.

5 CTS CORREOS MEXICO

CARL S. HELLIJAS, M.D.
HARTFORD HOSPITAL
80 SEYMOUR ST.
HARTFORD 6, CONN. U.S.A.

Lito en México.

Jamaica · Straw Market, Kingston (1968)

STRAW MARKET, Kingston, Jamaica

48

Dear Doctor:
    Here in Jamaica,
as almost everywhere
modern medicine is
practiced, you'll find
PENTOTHAL (thiopental).
Seldom in the history
of medicine has a
single drug achieved
greater world renown.
        Abbott

—————PENTOTHAL® SODIUM (Sodium Thiopental, Abbott)

PRINTED
MATTER

POSTAGE PAID

3d

KINGSTON
30 AUG
1 PM
1968
JAMAICA

DR ELIZ M FISHER
621 QUINBY AVE
WOOSTER OHIO 44691
U S A

Trinidad & Tobago · Piarco Airport, Trinidad (1967) · Card courtesy Tom Fortunato.

TIARCO AIRPORT, Trinidad, British W.I.

—————PENTOTHAL® SODIUM (Sodium Thiopental, Abbott)

PRINTED
MATTER

50

Dear Doctor:
    Trinidad, discovered
by Columbus in 1498,
has been welcoming
visitors ever since. One
visitor that has come
to stay is Pentothal—
an agent of choice here,
as in almost every
corner of the world.
        Abbott

DR ROY E WALLACE
32 CAYUGA ST
SENECA FALLS N Y   13148
U S A

United States · North Chicago Plant of Abbott Laboratories · Card only know to exist in Spanish.

NORTH CHICAGO PLANT OF ABBOTT LABORATORIES

Estimado Doctor:

52

Se han publicado más de 2300 trabajos sobre la anestesia intravenosa con Pentothal, desde que Abbott descubrió este agente en 1934. Dicho cúmulo de datos bibliográficos es un magnífico tributo a un fármaco desarrollado exclusivamente por un laboratorio comercial. Pero lo más importante es que constituye un sólido conjunto de antecedentes clínicos, que sirve de guía para usar el Pentothal con mayor seguridad, conveniencia y eficacia.

PENTOTHAL SÓDICO
Marca Registrada
(Tiopental Sódico Estéril, Abbott)

Abbott

D-11173

DR. P. MARTINEZ DOMINGO
BACACAY 3775
CAPITAL
ARGENTINA

Tours of the Abbott Laboritories are conducted by these Escorts of the Professional Guest Relations Department · Abbott Escorts.

54

Tours of Abbott Laboratories at North Chicago
are conducted by these Escorts of the Professional
Guest Relations Department.

Brown & Bigelow, Div. of Standard Packaging Corp., U.S.A.

613941

POST CARD

Equador · Children in Riobamba (1967)

ECUADOR: Niños en las calles de Riobamba.

56

Dear Nurse Anesthetist:
Here on the equator,
as in lands the world
around, the advantages
of PENTOTHAL (thiopental)
are familiar. Smooth and
painless administration,
easy maintenance, and
swift recovery make
PENTOTHAL an agent of
choice everywhere.
Abbott

PENTOTHAL® SODIUM (Sodium Thiopental, Abbott)

PRINTED
MATTER

CORREOS DEL ECUADOR GUAYAQUIL
8.3.67

KATHRYN L KELLY
17500 WESTMORELAND RD
DETROIT MICH 48219
U S A

Peru · Llamas (1965) · Even ruminant camelids need anesthesia.

58

Llamas en Perú. Escena de altiplano.

Dear Doctor:
 Truly PENTOTHAL
(thiopental) has made
itself the international
I.V. anesthetic. Here in Peru,
as in more than 100 other
lands around the globe,
PENTOTHAL is to be found
in daily service. Your own
patients can benefit from
this widely useful agent.
 Abbott

Swiss-Foto Lima

PENTOTHAL® SODIUM (Thiopental Sodium, Abbott)

DR CARL S HELLIJAS
4 RIVER RD
WETHERSFIELD CONN 06109
U S A

Brazil · National Congress (1963) · Built in 1958, the main architect was Oscar Niemeyer.

BRASILIA - DISTRITO FEDERAL - Brasil
CONGRESSO NACIONAL
CONGRÈS NATIONAL
THE NATIONAL CONGRESS

Dear Doctor:
    Yesterday only waist—high grasses of a trackless savanna stood here. Today sky scrapers thrust upward in one of the world's most advanced concepts of city planning. And as you would expect in Brasilia's ultramodern hospital operating rooms, PENTOTHAL (Thiopental) is an anesthetic of choice.
                Abbott

—PENTOTHAL® SODIUM (Thiopental Sodium, Abbott)——

PRINTED MAT⌐

DR. J. W. GILCHRIST
ONTARIO WORKMENS COMP. BD
90 HARBOUR ST.
TORONTO 1, ONT. CANADA.

P.B.-M. 5546

Columbia · Cartagena (1956)

62

CARTAGENA DE INDIAS (COLOMBIA)
VISTA DESDE EL CASTILLO DE SAN
FELIPE DE BARAJAS

TARJETA POSTAL

Dear Doctor:

More than 2300 reports in medical journals throughout the world have been published on intravenous anesthesia with Pentothal Sodium. Like their colleagues in other countries, doctors here in Colombia find that such exhaustive references, covering every aspect of anesthesia with Pentothal, mean greater convenience, safety and effectiveness in the employment of this powerful, short-acting agent.

Abbott

PENTOTHAL SODIUM
Trade Mark
(Sterile Thiopental Sodium, Abbott)

LITO CARVAJAL - CALI - COLOMBIA

CARTAGENA
1956
22 AGO
10.30
RECIBO

— COLOMB
PONGA LOS SELLOS

CORREOS DE COLOMBIA
INTENDENCIA DE SAN ANDRÉS Y PROVIDENCIA
PAISAJE DEL PUERTO
5 CENTAVOS 5
THOMAS DE LA RUE & CO LTD

LOUIS C. BLAHA, M.D.
245 E. 72ND ST.,
NEW YORK 21, N.Y.
U.S.A.

Venezuela · Picturesque view of the Gran Sabena · Venezuela has over 2,400 species of butterflies and moths.

64

Dear Doctor:

PENTOTHAL (thiopental) is one of the few names recognized almost everywhere that medicine is practiced. Here in Venezuela, as in more than 100 other lands the world around, PENTOTHAL is an intravenous agent of choice.

Abbott

LITO EN VENEZUELA

Koh K No.

—— PENTOTHAL® SODIUM (Sodium Thiopental, Abbott) ——

94C4P6

DR. CARL S. HELLIJAS,
4 RIVER RD.,
WETHERSFIELD, CONN. 06109
U. S. A.

Vnce

Columbia · Santa Marta (1964) · The world's highest coastal mountain range.

SANTA MARTA—COLOMBIA
Sierra Nevada

Dear Doctor:
    Snow-clad mountains are an everyday part of the Colombian scene. So, too, is PENTOTHAL (thiopental) an everyday part of the medical setting. Doctors here, as in 110 lands around the globe, know and trust this famous Abbott anesthetic.

        Abbott

PENTOTHAL® SODIUM (Thiopental Sodium, Abbott)

DIC 7 1964

BOGOTA - COLOM

COLOMBIA 10c

FERROCARRIL DEL ATLANTICO · 1961

DR. C.T.P. GARBUTT,
702 COXWELL AVE.,
TORONTO, ONT.
CANADA.

"Printed by Movifoto P.O. Box 12-54 Medellín-Colombia"

Chile · Rio Mapocho, Santiago (1964)

Río Mapocho, Santiago - CHILE

TARJETA POSTAL

68

Dear Nurse Anesthetist:

This unusual land stretches 2600 miles, yet averages only 100 miles wide. But in Chilean operating rooms you are on familiar ground again, for Pentothal is an every-day agent of choice here.

Abbott

112

MRS CARRIE B FISHER
527 W PENN ST
CARLISLE PA 17013
U S A

Argentina · Iguaza Falls (1964) · Iguazu–Guarani Indian word for great water.

Las espectaculares cascadas del Iguazú, entre Argentina y Brasil, descienden de una altura superior a la del salto del Niágara.

70

Dear Doctor:
   In the Argentine, too, PENTOTHAL (thiopental, Abbott) is a long time favorite. Among the reasons — PENTOTHAL is swift and brief in action. It produces unconsciousness in seconds. Degree of narcosis is readily controlled. Emergence is prompt.
   The same advantages are valid for your own hospital, doctor.
              Abbott

PENTOTHAL® SODIUM (Thiopental Sodium, Abbott)

DR. ROSS E. JOHNSTON,
2670 DANFORTH AVE.,
TORONTO 13, ONT.
CANADA.

Chile · Easter Island (1966) · Easter Island is also known as Rapa Nui, and is now the most isolated place on Earth.

72

EASTER ISLAND—The origin of these stone giants is a mystery that has intrigued many.

PENTOTHAL® SODIUM (Sodium Thiopental, Abbott)

Dear Doctor:
  Even here in lonely Easter Island, PENTOTHAL (thiopental) is known. Indeed, PENTOTHAL is one of the few names recognized almost everywhere that medicine is practiced. It is an intravenous agent of choice in lands the world around.
  Abbott

DR HARRY HERBERT BIRD
2 MAYNARD ST
HANOVER N H   03755
U S A

Nicaragua · Ruben Dario Monument, Managua (1968) · The poet Dario was born Félix Rubén García Sarmiento.

RUBEN DARIO MONUMENT
Managua, Nicaragua

74

Dear Nurse Anesthetist:
Nicaragua is
the largest state in
Central America. Here,
too, Pentothal is in
daily use. Its qualities
of simple administration,
easy control, and quick
recovery make it an
agent of choice.
Abbott

Photograph courtesy of Sawyer's Inc.

PENTOTHAL® SODIUM (Sodium Thiopental, Abbott)

LEONORE E FOSTER
1028 N 8TH ST
BURLINGTON IOWA   52601
U S A

Spanish Guinea · Bata, Rio (1963) · Bata is the largest city in Rio Muni, which is now part of Equitorial Guinea.

BATA, SPANISH GUINEA, AFRICA

76

Dear Doctor:
    American visitors to
this distant African land
are surprised to meet an
old friend: PENTOTHAL®
(Thiopental, Abbott) in
daily use. Yet there
should be no wonder.
The same qualities that
are appreciated here,
make this agent a
favorite the world
around: prompt, easy
induction and pleasant
uncomplicated recovery.
          Abbott

——PENTOTHAL® SODIUM (Thiopental Sodium, Abbott)——

MR. R.J. DUBOURDIEU, NO. 10
ABBOTT LABORATORIES,
14TH AND SHERIDAN ROAD,
NORTH CHICAGO, ILL. U.S.A.

Denmark · Little Mermaid (1957) · Den Lille Havfrue is a little over 4 feet tall, and weighs about 385 pounds.

COPENHAGEN: LANGELINIE
Edvard Eriksen's beautiful
sculpture illustrating
Hans Christian Andersen's fairy-tale
»The little Mermaid«.

78

Dear Doctor :

In Copenhagen, as wherever
modern surgery is practiced,
you'll find Pentothal Sodium in
constant use. More than
2700 published articles con-
firm these advantages: quick
response, moment to moment
control, smooth, painless induction and pleasant, swift
recovery.

PENTOTHAL SODIUM
Trade mark
(Sterile Thiopental Sodium, Abbott)

Abbott

T. C. BRERETON, M. D.
19 404 GRAHAM AVE.
WINNIPEG 1, MAN.
CANADA.

England · Nelson's Column, Trafalgar Square · Abbott UK was established in 1937 in Perivale, W. London.

Nelson's Column, Trafalgar Square
LONDON

80

Dear Doctor:

In England, too, Pentothal has been the subject of many medical papers. Indeed, Pentothal is the most widely studied agent of its kind the world around — with more than 4,000 published reports.

Abbott

NATURAL COLOUR SERIES
PHOTO
GREETINGS
U.S.A.

THE PHOTOGRAPHIC GREETING CARD CO. LTD., LONDON

PRINTED MATTER

PENTOTHAL® SODIUM (Sodium Thiopental, Abbott)
522

ARTIST UNKNOWN c.1575 HARRISON

4d

DR CARL S HELLIJAS
4 RIVER RD
WETHERSFIELD CONN   06109
U S A

France · Strasbourg (1957) · The white stork is the symbol of Alsace.

82

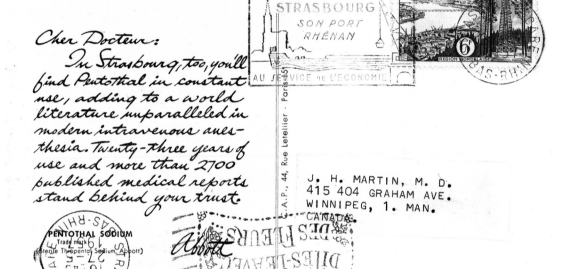

Cher Docteur:

In Strasbourg, too, you'll find Pentothal in constant use, adding to a world literature unparalleled in modern intravenous anesthesia. Twenty-three years of use and more than 2700 published medical reports stand behind your trust.

PENTOTHAL SODIUM
Trade mark
(Sterile Thiopental Sodium, Abbott)

STRASBOURG
SON PORT
RHÉNAN

AU SERVICE DE L'ÉCONOMIE

G.A.P., 44, Rue Letellier - Paris 15e

REPUBLIQUE FRANÇAISE
POSTES
6f
RÉGION BORDELAISE

J. H. MARTIN, M. D.
415 404 GRAHAM AVE.
WINNIPEG, 1. MAN.
CANADA

DITES-LE AVEC DES FLEURS
EN TOUTES CIRCONSTANCES

Abbott

England · Corfe Castle, Dorset (1958) · Built with Isle of Purbeck limestone.

CORFE CASTLE, DORSET
The castle ruins look down on the
old houses and inns of Corfe.

PRINTED MATTER

84

Dear Doctor:

One of the reasons doctors
here in England respect and
use PENTOTHAL is the
nearly 3000 published world
reports available to them for
reference. That, and a
clinical history of nearly
25 years. Good reasons, too,
for your trust.

Abbott

PENTOTHAL® SODIUM
(Thiopental Sodium for Injection, Abbott)

Printed in England

POOLE
20 AUG
1958

2d POSTAGE REVENUE 2d

Switzerland · Clock tower and statue · Swiss Confederation was founded in 1291.

86

Sehr geehrter Herr Doktor:

Yes, Pentothal is a favorite here in Switzerland, too — adding to a worldwide acceptance unmatched in modern intravenous anesthesia. 2700 published reports --and 23 years of use--stand behind its present unchallenged position!

PENTOTHAL® SODIUM
(Sterile Thiopental Sodium, Abbott)

Abbott

Photo Hch. Schellenberg, Zurich

BENJAMIN M. LEWIS, M.D.
WAYNE UNIVERSITY
COLLEGE OF MEDICINE
DETROIT 7, MICH, U.S.A.

Greece · View of the Parthenon on the Acropolis (1956) · Chief Temple of the goddess Athena, built in 447 BCE.

ATHENS - View of the
Parthenon on the Acropolis
seen from the Propylaeum

88

Dear Doctor,

Here in Athens, as wherever
modern surgery is practiced,
Pentothal Sodium continues to
grow in favor for intravenous
anesthesia. A solid background
of more than 2,300 articles
published in the world medical
press confirms Pentothal's
advantages: quick response,
moment to moment control,
smooth, painless induction
and pleasant, swift recovery.

PENTOTHAL SODIUM
Trade Mark
(Sterile Thiopental Sodium, Abbott)

Abbott

WINNIPEG MANITOBA
9 VI
4 PM
1956
CANADA

USE POST
ZONE NUMBER
ON ALL MAIL

J P Gutman M.D
100 Osborne Medical Bldg
100 Osborne St
Winnipeg
Man   Canada

Belgium · Grand Place (1966)

BRUXELLES : Un coin de la Grand'Place.
BRUSSEL : Een kijkje op de Grote Markt.
BRUSSELS : A part of the Market Place.

IMPRIME

Dear Nurse Anesthetist :

The Guild Halls of Brussels date back many years. In a medical sense PENTOTHAL (thiopental) offers a long history too. Its successful clinical experience of more than 30 years is unmatched among I.V. anesthetics. No wonder it is an agent of choice, not only in Belgium but in lands the world around

Abbott

89
PENTOTHAL® SODIUM (Thiopental Sodium, Abbott)

PRINTED IN BELGIUM

MRS. SARAH S. PONESMITH
206 BOSLER AVE.
LEMOYNE, PA.
U.S.A.

France · Montmartre (1964)
 Thujone is derived from wormwood leaves in the preparation of the liquor absinthe. It exacerbated van Gogh's porphyria.

IV - PARIS
The Eiffel Tower

PRINTED MATTER
(IMPRIMÉ)
DIEPPE
29_30
mar

CONFÉRENCE du 164e DISTRICT
ROTARY INTERNATIONAL

REPUBLIQUE FRANÇAISE
GASTON RAMON
2e CENTENAIRE DE L'ÉCOLE VÉTÉRINAIRE D'ALFORT
0.25

Dear Doctor :

Greetings from the heart of France! Here in Paris PENTOTHAL (thiopental) is probably as well-known as it is in your own hospital. But small wonder. More than 4000 world reports have now been published on PENTOTHAL. It is unquestionably the most widely studied agent of its kind.

Abbott

—— PENTOTHAL® SODIUM (Sodium Thiopental)

Carl S Helligas MD
4 River Rd
Wethersfield Conn 06109
U. S. A.

Spain · Vista parcial del Puerto de Palos · The harbor has silted up since 1492.

94

Dear Doctor:
From this Spanish port, Columbus first set sail for America. To Spain from America, in turn, has come PENTOTHAL (thiopental). In hospitals here, as in America, it is prized for its ease of administration, its speed of action, and its many years of clinical use.

Abbott

—PENTOTHAL® SODIUM (Thiopental Sodium, Abbott)—

DR. ARTHUR C. HARDMAN,
19 NANAIMO DRIVE,
BELLS CORNERS, ONT.
CANADA.

R.M.S. "Queen Elizabeth"

England · R.M.S. *Queen Elizabeth* (1959) · The maiden passenger voyage was in October, 1946.

R.M.S. Queen Elizabeth (The Cunard Steam-Ship Company Ltd.) is of 83,673 tons gross, is 1031′ 0″ long and 118′ 7″ wide. She carries over 2,000 passengers and is the largest liner in the world.

96

"At sea"

Dear Doctor:

Every comfort is provided aboard the R. M. S. Queen Elizabeth, including first-rate medical care. The ship's doctors demand -- and get -- the utmost in dependability and safety in their medical supplies. One of their choices is PENTOTHAL -- agent of choice the world over in intravenous anesthesia.

Abbott

PENTOTHAL® SODIUM
(Thiopental Sodium for Injection, Abbott)

DR. WILLARD S. SMALL,
960 E. GREEN ST.,
PASADENA 1, CALIF.
U. S. A.

SOUTHAMPTON
1 30 PM
17 SEP
1959
B

Ireland · O'Connell Street, Dublin City (1956) · This is one of the widest streets in Europe.

98

O'CONNELL STREET, DUBLIN CITY
Down the centre of this fine street are situated the O'Connell
and Parnell monuments, the Statue of Father
Theobald Mathew and the Nelson Pillar.

Dear Doctor,

More than 2,300 reports in
medical journals throughout
the world have been published
on intravenous anesthesia with
Pentothal Sodium. Like their
colleagues in other countries,
doctors here in Éire find that
such exhaustive references,
covering every aspect of anesthesia
with Pentothal, mean greater
convenience, safety and effectiveness
in the employment of this
powerful, short-acting agent.

PENTOTHAL SODIUM
Trade Mark
(Sterile Thiopental Sodium, Abbott)

Abbott

R. G. Maxwell, M.D.
420 Medical Art Bldg.
Winnipeg
Man   Canada

Lundy · Horses and lighthouse (1962) · The lighthouse symbolizes vigilance.

100

PRINTED MATTER RATE

HAVE YOU
TAKEN OUT
YOUR LICEN...
FOR RADIO...

Doctor,
    We've found it at last!
A place without PENTOTHAL!
Lundy island is a self-
governing dominion about 1.6
miles square; has its own
stamps, puffin and half-
puffin, and coins, but
no hospitals.   Happily,
Lundy is about 12 miles
away from another island —
England — so the islanders
don't have to go far to receive
the finest hospital care — and
of course PENTOTHAL, the worldwide intravenous anesthetic
of choice.
                        Abbott

PENTOTHAL® (Thiopental, Abbott)

A

DR. CHARLES J. BRIM,
901 WALTON AVE.,
NEW YORK 52, N. Y.
U.S.A.

Malta · Old fortification of Valletta (1965)

MALTA—Old fortification of Valletta,
overlooking sailing craft on the Mediterranean.

102

Dear Doctor:
    Since the Crusades,
Malta has played an
important role in war and
peace. Today in Maltese
medical practice, PENTOTHAL
(thiopental) too plays an
important role. Here, as in
lands around the globe,
the reliability of PENTOTHAL
is appreciated.
           Abbott

PENTOTHAL® SODIUM (Thiopental Sodium, Abbott)

DR C S HELLIJAS
4 RIVER RD
WETHERSFIELD CONN 06109
U.S.A.

Germany · Berlin: Congress-hall and the river Spree (1963)
Designed by Hugh Stubbins as the American contribution to the International Building Exhibition in 1957.

"BERLIN: Kongresshalle und Spree
congress-hall and the river Spree"

104

Dear Doctor:
    In this divided city,
PENTOTHAL is no longer to be
found on the other side of the
Wall. But here in West Berlin
(as in every major world city
outside the Iron Curtain)
PENTOTHAL is known, trusted,
and used. Its record for safety,
effectiveness, and versatility are
unsurpassed in I.V. anesthesia.
                    Abbott

—PENTOTHAL® SODIUM (Thiopental Sodium·Abbott)

ein Postfach
dann schreib
an sein
Postfach!

BERLIN 11

DR. NANCY BEATTIE,
T.B. CONRTROL, HAMILTON
74 HUGHSON ST. S.
HAMILTON, ONT. CANADA.

264

San Marino · View of Castle (1958) · Founded by Marinus the Dalmation, 301 CE.

REPUBBLICA DI S. MARINO
Panorama   *View*
Vue   *Ansicht*

106

Dear Doctor:
Here in San Marino,
PENTOTHAL is probably
as well known as it is
in your own hospital.
Nearly 3000 world reports
is one reason. An excellent
safety record is another.
Good reasons, too, for
your trust.
Abbott

PENTOTHAL® SODIUM
(Thiopental Sodium for Injection, Abbott)

REP. DI S. MARINO   LIRE 15

DR. HERMAN N. HAMILTON,
ARKANSAS CHILDREN'S HOSP.
804 WOLFE ST.,
LITTLE ROCK, ARK. U.S.A.

EUROPEA - ROMA

Germany · Gœthehaus Frankfurt am Main (1957) · Gœthe could speak 6 languages; his sister 3.

GOETHEHAUS FRANKFURT AM MAIN (GERMANY)

108

Sehr geehrter Herr Doktor:

To date, more than 2700 articles on Pentothal Sodium have appeared in the world medical press, including many journals here in Germany. This imposing bibliography has made Pentothal Sodium practically synonymous with modern intravenous anesthesia...and helps explain why Pentothal continues to grow in favor as an agent of choice.

PENTOTHAL® SODIUM
(Sterile Thiopental Sodium, Abbott)

Abbott

ALFRED J. BOLLET, M.D.
WAYNE UNIV. COLL. OF MED.
1401 RIVARD ST.
DETROIT 7, MICH. U. S. A.

Portugal · Monument of the Discoveries in Belém (1961) · Behind the Prince are other Portuguese heroes.

Monument of the Discoveries in Belém, outside Lisbon, commemorates the 500th anniversary of Prince Henry the Navigator, pioneer of maritime discovery.

Dear Doctor:

Here in Portugal, our special stamp commemorates the life 5 centuries ago, of Prince Henry the Navigator. Today PENTOTHAL too has charted new worlds of progress. You'll like its dependable, easily controlled intravenous anesthesia. Use it soon.

Abbott

PENTOTHAL® (Thiopental, Abbott)

A

INDAGUE NO
COMO ENDERE
RECTAMENTE
CORRESPOND

Hi— "you all"!
Best regards, believe me. Ben

DR. BEN L. BEAR,
1642 SAN GABRIEL AVE.,
GLENDALE 8, CALIF.,
U. S. A.

Netherlands · Madurodam (1965) · Modeled after Bekonscot, Beaconsfield, UK.

MADURODAM
Dutch city in miniature, painstakingly reproduced
at 1/20th scale, charms visitors young or old.

112

Geachte Heer Dokter:
Here in the Netherlands,
PENTOTHAL (thiopental)
is a regular feature of
operating rooms. It is
well liked for its quick,
brief action — with smooth,
easy induction and prompt
recovery. These same
qualities can serve you
well in your own operating
room.
Abbott

——— PENTOTHAL® SODIUM (Thiopental Sodium, Abbott)

SOCIAAL EN
CULTUREEL WERK
DOOR ZOMERZEGELS
STERK

NEDERLAND 10c

DR WILFRED DERBYSHIRE
70 PRINCESS ST
FORT ERIE ONT
CANADA

Luxembourg · Chateau de Vianden (1958) · The castle is now restored to its former glory.

114

Dear Doctor

Here in Luxembourg, PENTOTHAL is probably as well known as it is in your own hospital. Nearly 3000 world reports is one reason. An excellent safety record is another. Good reasons, too, for your trust.

Abbott

PENTOTHAL® SODIUM
(Thiopental Sodium for Injection, Abbott)

CHATEAU DE VIANDEN
GRAND-DUCHÉ DE LUXEMBOURG
(Photo M. Schroeder, Lxbg)

Vianden joyau des Ardennes

POSTE AERIENNE
1F
LUXEMBOURG

Monaco · View of the port at night (1967) · Grace Kelly married Prince Rainier of Monaco on April 18, 1956.

Monaco — View of the port at night,
showing the casino and pool of Rainier III

IMPRIMÉ

116

PENTOTHAL® SODIUM (Sodium Thiopental)

Dear Doctor:

Even in this tiny principality, the advantages of PENTOTHAL (thiopental) are familiar. Smooth and painless induction, easy maintenance, and swift recovery make PENTOTHAL an agent of choice the world around. Your Abbott representative will be glad to help you arrange for PENTOTHAL in your own hospital.

Abbott

DR. CARL S. HELLIJAS,
4 RIVER RD.,
WETHERSFIELD, CONN. 06109
U. S. A.

Finland · Children's Castle (1958) · Architects—Borg, Flodin & Sortta.

Helsinki – Helsingfors
Lastenlinna
Barnensborg
The Children's Castle

118

Dear Doctor:
After 24 years, PENTOTHAL
still grows in world wide
use. Indeed, many doctors
here in Finland - like their
colleagues the world over-
think of PENTOTHAL as
synonymous with intra-
venous anesthesia. Their
reasons: Safety..Versatility.

Abbott

PENTOTHAL SODIUM
Trade Mark
(Thiopental Sodium for Injection, Abbott)

Printed in Sweden   Bengtsons Litografiska AB

USA

CALIF. MENS COLONY,
SAN LUIS OBISPO,
CALIFORNIA,
U.S.A.

Andorra · House of Parliament (1958) · Income tax free in the Pyrenees since 1278.

120

Dear Doctor:

You won't find many doctors in the world that don't know about PENTOTHAL. Certainly, here in Andorra they know about PENTOTHAL — they use it all the time! They particularly like PENTOTHAL's safety and versatility — two points that rank high in any part of the world.

Abbott

PENTOTHAL® SODIUM
(Thiopental Sodium for Injection, Abbott)

ANDORRE LA VIEILLE: MAISON DU PARLEMENT

EDICIONES CASTILLA, S. A. - MADRID

DUBLIN

Ireland · County Dublin (1967)

122

Dear Nurse Anesthetist:
Good friends are easy to find in the Emerald Isle. In the hospitals, for example, you'll find a familiar friend: Pentothal—popular here for the same sensible reasons as back home.

Abbott

PENTOTHAL® SODIUM
(Sodium Thiopental, Abbott)

PRINTED MATTER

COUNTY DUBLIN. Dublin—beautiful, entertaining, witty Dublin, city of Sean O'Casey, James Joyce George Bernard Shaw, Sheridan, Swift and a host of other wizards with words—as indeed, is the average Dubliner; city of the largest stout brewery, largest urban park, highest obelisk, oldest Chamber of Commerce. Dublin is one of the most beautifully-situated of the world's capitals, between the mountains and the sea, with unspoiled countryside lapping at its doorstep. It is friendly, loquacious, hospitable and gracious.

Printed and Published by John Hinde Limited, Cabinteely, Co. Dublin, Irish Republic.

MRS SARAH S PONESMITH
205 HOSLER AVE
LEMOUNE PA 17043
U S A

Italy · Ponte di Rialto, Venice (1957) · Designed by Antonio da Ponte in 1588.

VENEZIA

Ponte di Rialto   Rialto - Bridge
Pont de Rialto   Rialtobrücke

124

Egregio Dottore:

From Italy and from all parts of
the world where modern surgery is
practiced comes a steady flow of
published reports confirming the
advantages of intravenous anesthesia with Pentothal. Among them:

Smooth, rapid induction
Easily-controlled levels
Short, uncomplicated
recovery

Abbott

PENTOTHAL® SODIUM
(Sterile Thiopental Sodium, Abbott)

ALTEROCCA
TERNI

PRINTED IN ITALY

RICHARD C. WIXSON, M.D.
110 E. MAIN ST.
MADISON 3, WIS.
U.S.A.

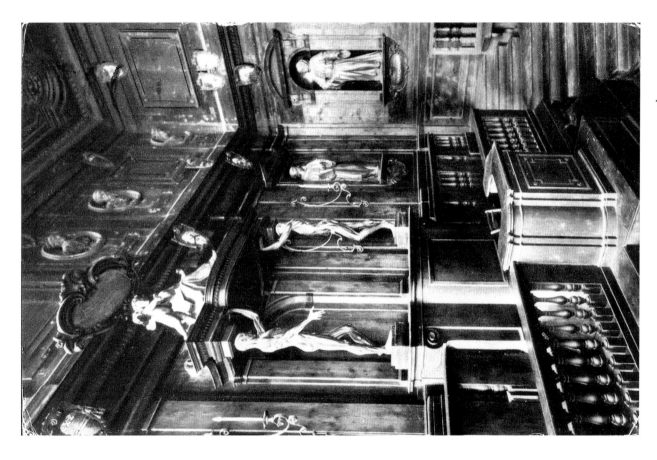

Italy · University of Bologna (1961) · University of Bologna was founded in 1088.

UNIVERSITÀ DI BOLOGNA
(la più antica d'Europa)
Aula Magna con Cattedra e Sculture in legno (Sec. XVII)

Dear Doctor:
The University of
Bologna is the home
of one of Europe's oldest
medical schools. Here
PENTOTHAL is pronounced
an anesthetic of choice.
You, too, will approve
its easy induction,
dependable control, and
swift recovery.
Abbott

PENTOTHAL® (Thiopental, Abbott)

A

DR. ERIC F. A. STEINTHAL
144 DUBOIS ST.,
NEWBURGH, N. Y.
U. S. A.

Liechtenstein · Children in native dress · Card courtesy Henry Ratz.

128

II - LIECHTENSTEIN
Children in Native Dress

Zum
Wintersport
nach
LIECHTENSTEIN

FVERSTENTVM
LIECHTENSTEIN
20

PENTOTHAL® SODIUM (Sodium Thiopental, Abbo

Dear Doctor:

Liechtenstein is an independent principality with an unusual distinction: its citizens are virtually without taxes. Though this nation on the upper Rhine is tiny, you will find PENTOTHAL (thiopental) in regular use by physicians here. Indeed, PENTOTHAL is a familiar agent of choice in scores of lands large and small, the world around!

Abbott

Chandler Sparkman Smith MD
2217 Webster St
San Francisco Calif 94115
U.S.A

India · Taj Mahal, Agra (1966) · Mumtaz Mahal was born Arjumand Banu, in 1593.

The TAJ MAHAL — Agra, India: Built by the emperor Shah Jahan as a memorial to his queen.

130

Dear Doctor:

The Taj Mahal is justly world-famed. So, too, PENTOTHAL (thiopental) has justly become the world's best-known agent of its kind. It is a subject of more than 4,000 published world reports. No wonder PENTOTHAL has become an agent of choice in more than 100 lands the world around.

Abbott

POST CARD

BY SEA MAIL

DR AUGUST C MAZZA
2311 S MAIN ST
FINDLAY OHIO 45840
U S A

Jordan · Dome of the rock, Jerusalem.

DOME OF THE ROCK on a Jerusalem hilltop
site traditionally revered by major religions.

132

Dear Doctor:
    Here in Jerusalem
as in every major city
outside the Iron Curtain,
PENTOTHAL (thiopental)
anesthesia is in daily
use. Its simplicity of
administration, speed of
action, and pleasant
recovery can easily make
PENTOTHAL a valued agent
in your own practice.
                    Abbott

PENTOTHAL® SODIQUE (Thiopental Sodique, Abbott)

PRINTED IN LEBANON — MEEPI

PRINTE

19 NANAIMO DRIVE
BELLS CORNERS, C
DA.

Lebanon · Byblos (1963) · Ancient Phoenician city, now Jubayl.

BYBLOS, LEBANON
The history of this sunny Mediterranean
port dates back into the pre-Christian era.

134

Dear Doctor:
Greetings from Byblos,
Lebanon — a contender for
the title of the oldest
continuously inhabited city
on earth! Old, yet modern,
too — for in the local clinic
PENTOTHAL® (Thiopental,
Abbott) is well known.
Ease of administration,
freedom from delirium,
and recovery without
complications make this
agent a favorite the
world around.
                    Abbott

PENTOTHAL® SODIUM (Thiopental Sodium, Abbott)

PRINTED MATTER

5 P. **LIBAN**
POSTE AERIENNE

DR. H. B. PARLEE,
142 CHARLOTTE ST.,
ST. JOHN, N. B.
CANADA

PRINTED IN LEBANON — MEEPI

Malaya Selangor · Malay mosque, Kuala Lumpur (1964) · Malasia was formed in 1963.

A MALAY MOSQUE
Kuala Lumpur

Dear Doctor:

In this busy, modern Malaysian city, PENTOTHAL (thiopental) anesthesia is well known by physicians. The speed of induction, absence of delirium, ease of control, and rapid emergence have made this anesthetic popular. Ask your Abbott man about PENTOTHAL for your own hospital practice.

Abbott

PENTOTHAL® SODIUM (Thiopental Sodium, Abbott)

DR. CHARLES L. MACLELLAN,
BISHOP BLOCK,
SYDNEY, N. S.
CANADA

PRINTED MATTER

Maldive Islands · Minaret of Juma Mosque, Male (1962) · Hukuru Miskiiy, for Juma (Friday) prayers.

MINARET OF JUMA MOSQUE
IN MALE, MALDIVE ISLANDS

138

Dear Doctor:

    If you've been looking for a far-away island paradise, you'll find it in the Maldive Islands. The Islands are just south of the great Indian peninsula. While few westerners visit here, and the best means of transportation is by sailing ship, you will always find PENTOTHAL. Its sureness, effectiveness, and solid clinical background have made it the intravenous anesthetic of choice throughout the world.

                     Abbott

—PENTOTHAL® (Thiopental, Abbott)——

A

PRINTED MATTER

DR. MOHAMED R. HAGHIGH,
2355 EUTAW PL.,
BALTIMORE 17, MD.,
U. S. A.

Thailand · Scenery of Pagoda of Dawn, Dhonburi (1963) · Wat Arun, Temple of the Dawn, faces Bangkok.

ธนบุรี พระปรางค์ใหญ่แห่งวัดอรุณ.

DHONBURI, THAILAND: Scenery of Pagoda of Dawn is a unique example of Thai decorative art.

140

Dear Doctor:

This colorful, friendly city possesses many fine hospitals. In them you'll find PENTOTHAL (Thiopental, Abbott) in daily use. Doctors here like its simplicity of administration, its versatility, and its long record of experience. Good reasons, too, for your own preference for PENTOTHAL!

Abbott

PENTOTHAL® SODIUM (Thiopental Sodium, Abbott)

MR. ALFRED D'ANNIBALLE,
6475 ANITA DR.,
PARMA HEIGHTS 30, OHIO
U. S. A.

Japan · National Park, Hakone (1959) · Torii gate, Lake Ashi, Mt. Fuji.

National Park, Hakone, Japan

国立公園 ● 箱　根

142

Dear Doctor:
In Japan, as wheriver modern medicine is practiced, PENTOTHAL'S advantages continue to make it an agent of choice. Among the advantages doctors here like are quick response, smooth, painless induction and an uncomplicated, yet swift recovery.

Abbott

PENTOTHAL® SODIUM
(Thiopental Sodium for Injection, Abbott)

PRINTED IN JAPAN.

1959

DR. ELLEN SOO SUN SONG,
BEVERLY HOSPITAL
HERRICK-HEATHER STS.,
BEVERLY, MASS., U.S.A.

Pakistan · Shalamar Gardens, Lahore (1967) · East Pakistan became Bangladesh in 1971.

144

Dear Nurse Anesthetist:

1000 miles of intervening foreign lands separate the two parts of this nation. But in East and West Pakistan alike, operating room teams agree on the merits of Pentothal.

Abbott

PENTOTHAL® SODIUM (Sodium Thiopental, Abbott)

*PRINTED BY PACKAGES LTD. LAHORE, PAKISTAN ©

BY AIR MAIL

PRINTED MATTER

POST CARD

POSTAGE PAISA 10 PAKISTAN

RICE WE EXPORT THE BEST

50 PAISA POSTAGE PAKISTAN

DEC 25 1966

KATHRYN L KELLY
17500 WESTMORELAND
DETROIT MICH 48219
U S A

Pakistan · Ilyasi Mosque, Abbottabad (1964) · Sir James Abbott settled Hazara in 1853.

ABBOTTABAD, PAKISTAN
Ilyasi Mosque, whose underground springs flow
hot in winter, cold in summer, is a century-old
landmark in this modern Pakistani city.

146

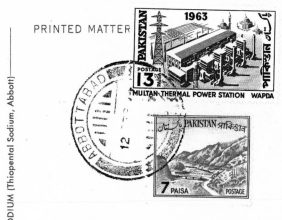

Dear Doctor:
Abbottabad City is
named in honor of a man
called Abbott. Sorry, not
related to us. However
Abbott products such as
PENTOTHAL® (Thiopental)
are well-known in
Abbottabad. This agent's
smooth induction, reliable
response, and swift
recovery are appreciated
here . . . as in cities
around the world.
Abbott

— PENTOTHAL® SODIUM (Thiopental Sodium, Abbott)

DR. ROBERT B. MEIKLEJOHN,
TORONTO WESTERN HOSPITAL,
399 BATHURST ST.
TORONTO 2B, ONT.   CANADA.

Hong Kong · Cargo junks in Hong Kong harbor (1960)

148

CARGO JUNKS IN HONG KONG HARBOUR

PRINTED PAPER

CORRECT ADDRESS
SAVES

Dear Doctor:
    East meets West
in busy Hong Kong.
And here, as elsewhere,
clinicians prefer drugs
with a well-established
record of effectiveness
and safety. Of course,
they choose PENTOTHAL
- the intravenous
anesthetic used
around the world.

                    Abbott

DR. JAMES SMALL
306 KING ST.
MIDLAND, ONT.
CANADA

India · Victoria Terminus, Bombay (1967) · Bombay's Victoria Terminus is now Chhatrapati Shivaji Terminus, Mumbai.

VICTORIA TERMINUS—BOMBAY: Completed in 1888,
V.T. is one of the biggest Railway Terminals of the East.

150

Dear Doctor:
    Here in exotic
India, as the world
around, Pentothal continues
to grow in favor among
operating room personnel.
Over 4000 published
world reports now attest
to the efficacy of
Pentothal.
      Abbott

PENTOTHAL® SODIUM (Sodium Thiopental, Abbott)

PRINTED MATTER

BY SEA

DR CARL S HELLIJAS
4 RIVER RD
WETHERSFIELD CONN 06109
U S A

Ceylon · Snake charmer with Cobra (1960)

Ceylon: Snake Charmer with Cobra

152

Ceylon, land of contrast. In its remote areas lived the Veddas, a primitive folk probably direct descendants of an ancient civilization. But there is another Ceylon, of modern stores, fine hospitals. In them you'll find PENTOTHAL—agent of choice in intravenous anesthesia the world over.

Abbott

De Soysa & Co. Limited, Colombo.

PRINTED MATTER

PENTOTHAL® (Thiopental Abbott)

MRS. BEVERLY LATTIMER,
324 N. MADISON,
MASON CITY, IOWA
U. S. A.

Surinam · Governments Plein, Paramaribo (1960) · Surinam became independent in 1975.

SURINAM—Governments Plein, Paramaribo.

PHOTO COURTESY ALCOA STEAMSHIP CO.

154

Dear Doctor:
Here, in tropical Surinam, doctors want and need, an intra-venous anesthetic that will assure an uncomplicated, swift recovery. They find it in PENTOTHAL --- agent of choice the world over.

Abbott

—PENTOTHAL® (Thiopental, Abbott)

A

Singapore · Riverfront, downtown Singapore (1962) · Singapore left Malaysia in 1965.

156

Dear Doctor:

Singapore combines the glamour of the Orient with all the comforts of home. Medical care is tops. Singapore has some of the best equipped hospitals in the Far East. And, as in other modern cities, you'll always find safe, predictable PENTOTHAL — unmistakably, the world's most widely studied intravenous anesthetic.

Abbott

50¢

PENTOTHAL® (Thiopental, Abbott)

A

HIPPOCAMPUS KUDA

2 CENTS **SINGAPORE**

6 CENTS **SINGAPORE**

HIPPOCAMPUS KUDA

2 CENTS **SINGAPORE**

30 JUNE

DR. GERHARD B. HAUGEN
1020 S.W. TAYLOR ST.
PORTLAND 5, OREG.
U.S.A.

Hong Kong · Hong Kong by Night (1963)

158

PRINTED PAPER

HONG KONG BY NIGHT

Dear Doctor:

Colorful lights of busy ferries streak the harbor between Kowloon and Hong Kong. In this bustling metropolis — as in every major city outside the Iron Curtain — doctors daily use PENTOTHAL (Thiopental, Abbott). It is unmistakably the world's most widely used intravenous anesthetic.

Abbott

HONG KONG
27 JUN
1963
A

PENTOTHAL (Thiopental, Abbott) COLOR PHOTOGRAPH BY

15¢ HONG KONG

Taiwan · Pineapple cart, Hualien (1966)

Pineapple cart returning home fully laden.
Hualien, Taiwan

Dear Doctor:
This oriental island is some 7,000 miles from America. Yet PENTOTHAL (thiopental) is well-known to Taiwan doctors. Small wonder. PENTOTHAL's time-tested virtues have made it a favorite the world around.

Abbott

—— PENTOTHAL® SODIUM (Thiopental Sodium, Abbott) ——

DR WILFRED DERBYSHIRE
70 PRINCESS ST
FORT ERIE ONT
CANADA

Ruanda–Urundi · Animals and mountains (1959) · The Tutsi people tower over the tiny Twa cattle.

162

Dear Doctor:

Here in Ruanda-Urundi, you'll find men who grow to be seven feet tall. And you'll also find doctors here using the latest in modern medical techniques... and of course, PENTOTHAL. Surgeons the world over think of PENTOTHAL as synonymous with intravenous anesthesia.

Abbott.

PENTOTHAL® SODIUM
(Thiopental Sodium for Injection, Abbott)

" Cliché : CONGO TOURISME ,,

11-II 1960

DR. JAMES A. STANSFIELD
QUINCY,
WASHINGTON
U.S.A.

129

Comoro Islands · Group of women in native costume.

COMORES
(group of women in native costume)

164

Printed
in
France

MUTS. MUDU
10 -6
1965
COMORES

COMORES

Dear Doctor:

Greetings and good Anesthesia from the Comoro Islands! The Comoros are tiny, remote jewels in the Mozambique Channel of the Indian Ocean. Yet PENTOTHAL (Thiopental) has found its way here, as to lands large and small around the globe. Truly PENTOTHAL has become the international I.V. agent.

Abbott.

C. Landry

Wilfred Derbyshire, M.D.
70 Princes St.,
Fort Erie. Ont.
Canada.

PENTOTHAL® SODIUM (Thiopental Sodium Abbott)

South Africa · Venda native women (1958)

PRINTED MATTER

Dear Doctor:

~~Here in South Africa~~
PENTOTHAL is probably
as well known as it is in
your hospital. Nearly 3000
world reports is one reason.
An excellent safety record
is another. Good reasons,
too, for your trust.

Abbott

PENTOTHAL® SODIUM
(Thiopental Sodium for Injection, Abbott)

DR. STANLEY R. PARKINSON,
326 "G" ST.,
MARYSVILLE, CALIF.
U. S. A.

©C.T. LTD.   Venda Native Women, South Africa.

Kenya · Greetings from East Africa (1967) · Formerly part of British East Africa.

168

Dear Nurse Anesthetist:
    Kenya, independent
since 1963, is one of
more than 100 lands
old and new where
Pentothal is used.
Simple administration,
easy control, and quick
recovery make Pentothal
a favorite around the
world.
                Abbott

PENTOTHAL® SODIUM (Sodium Thiopental, Abbott)

N. 281

COME TO THE
JAMHURI PARK
PRINTED

THOMSON'S
GAZELLE
KENYA 5c

ANT BEAR
KENYA 15c

LT COL MARJORIE CONLY
BOX 353 LETTERMAN HOSP
SAN FRANCISCO CAL   94129
U S A

Sidi Ifni · Plaza de España, Sidi Ifni (1959)
      Sidi Ifni was returned to Morocco by Spain in 1969, 13 years after the rest of Morocco got its independence.

170

Dear Doctor:

In tiny Ifni, PENTOTHAL'S advantages continue to make it an agent of choice in intravenous anesthesia. Among these advantages; quick response, smooth, painless induction and an uncomplicated, yet swift recovery.

Abbott

PENTOTHAL® SODIUM
(Thiopental Sodium for Injection, Abbott)

PLAZA DE ESPAÑA. - SIDI IFNI

DR. ERICH BAENDER,
116 W. MERRICK ST.,
FREEPORT, L.I., N.Y.,
U. S. A.

PRINTED MATTER

Philippines · Ifugao village in Banaue, Mt. Province (1966)
H. Otley Beyer, the anthropologist and archaeologist, was buried in the hills of Banaue in 1966.

IFUGAO VILLAGE IN BANAUE, MT. PROVINCE —
Considered the 8th wonder of the world are these
rice fields carved from the mountain sides with
primitive tools in the Philippines.

172

Dear Doctor :
  Here in the Philippines,
PENTOTHAL (thiopental) is in
daily use by anesthesiologists.
It is well-liked because
of its easy administration,
quick response, moment-to-
moment control, and pleasant
recovery. Your own practice
can benefit from these
same advantages.
                Abbott

PENTOTHAL® SODIUM (Sodium Thiopental, Abbott)

PRINTED IN U.S.A.

DR. WILFRED DERBYSHIRE,
70 PRINCESS ST.,
FORT ERIE, ONT.,
CANADA

PRINTED MATTER

Australia · Ayers Rock, N.T. (1967) · Ayers Rock.

Ayers Rock, N.T.
This aerial view of Ayers Rock, the largest monolith in the world, also shows the Olgas, 20 miles west of Ayers Rock. "Uluru" is the aboriginal name for Ayers Rock, which has been used by their ancestors for carving of their many legends and myths. It is 300 miles south-west of Alice Springs, rising from the flat surrounding area to 1,143 ft., 2,820 ft. above sea level and 5-1/2 miles around its base. Ayers Rock was named after the S.A. Premier, Sir Henry Ayers.

174

——— PENTOTHAL® SODIUM (Sodium Thiopental, ﹐

Dear Doctor:

Greetings from down under! Here in Australia, too, you'll find Pentothal. Over 30 years of worldwide clinical experience have today given it a background unmatched in its field.

Abbott

POST CARD

−1 SE 67
CENTRAL
AUSTRALIA

AYERS ROCK — ONE OF THE WORLD'S LARGEST MONOLITH

DR CARL S RELLIJAS
4 RIVER RD
WETHERSFIELD CONN   06109
U S A

Sweden · Laplandish fall and spring living quarters (1958) · Lapland has a high incidence of porphyria.

Lapskt höst- och vårviste, Tarradalen, Jokkmokk.
Laplandish fall and spring living quarters, Tarradalen
(the Valley of Tarra), Jokkmokk.

176

Even here in Polcirkeln,
Sweden, on the Arctic
Circle, PENTOTHAL is a
familiar and valued "agent
of choice." In fact, there's
hardly a city or country
in the civilized world
that doesn't know and
use PENTOTHAL. And a
literature of 3000 world
reports confirms it!

PENTOTHAL® SODIUM
(Thiopental Sodium for Injection, Abbott)

Abbott

Printed in Sweden JII Tre Tryckare A571-1578 Foto Gunnar Rönn

MRS. RUTH D. TEBO
3831 ARNOLD ST.
HOUSTON 5, TEX.
U.S.A.

Fiji · Police Force Fanfare Trumpeters (1967) · Card courtesy Tom Fortunato.

FIJI POLICE FORCE FANFARE TRUMPETERS

The proud traditions of the Fiji Police Force are given colour and expression in this striking study of Police Trumpeters who figure on important ceremonial occasions in Fiji. These Trumpeters typify the proud bearing, dignity and smart appearance of the Force whose unique uniform is not seen anywhere else in the World.

H. S. EKTACHROME BY CHARLES STINSON

178

Dear Doctor:

There are 322 Fiji Islands. 216 aren't inhabited. But in the other 106 Pentothal has become a familiar medical agent. Indeed, almost no corner of the earth is too remote to find Pentothal.

Abbott

PENTOTHAL® SODIUM (Sodium Thiopental, Abbott)

DR ROY E WALLACE
32 CAYUGA ST
SENECA FALLS N Y   13148
U S A

Wallis and Futuna · Wallis et Futuna (1965) · Samuel Wallis renamed Uvea after himself.

180

WALLIS ET FUTUNA
(deux groupes d'îles tropicales entre Fidji et Samoa)

Greetings Doctor:

Did you not know about the beautiful Wallis and Futuna archipelago? Then come and visit here. The populace (all 9,900 of them) will warmly welcome you to this Polynesian paradise. What's more you'll find an old friend serving in the clinic. Yes, PENTOTHAL (thiopental) - truly an agent of choice the world around.

Abbott

Photo C. Landry

PENTOTHAL® SODIUM (Thiopental Sodium, Abbott)

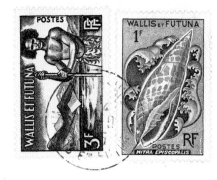

Carl S. Hellijas MD

4 River Rd

Wethersfield Conn 06109

U.S.A.

IMPRIMÉ

French Polynesia · Beach scene, Tahiti (1965) · AKA Otaheite or King George III Island.

TAHITI—Beach scene

182

Dear Doctor:

In this sunlit South Pacific isle, PENTOTHAL (thiopental) serves. Here, as in almost every part of the globe, its advantages are well known. Easy administration. Smooth induction. Predictable narcosis. Swift recovery. These same merits can serve well in your own practice.

Abbott

PENTOTHAL® SODIUM (Thiopental Sodium, Abbott)

IMPRIMÉE R.P.

PAPEETE R.P. ILE TAHITI 3-3 1965

PAPEETE ILE T. 3 1965

John B. Mc Collough
184, Rolling Hills Road
Elkins Pk.
Philadelphia — Pennsylv. 1917
USA.

New Hebrides · Native (1966) · New Hedrides became Vanuatu in 1980.

IMPRIMÉ

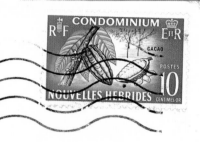

A native of the New Hebrides, in the South Pacific. VILA

Dear Doctor:

In these islands of the Coral Sea, life is still in transition from the old to new. One of the greatest changes has been the arrival of modern medical care — including, of course, PENTOTHAL (thiopental). Indeed, this familiar I.V. agent is now at home in every corner of the world.

Abbott

Photo C. Landry

PENTOTHAL® SODIUM (Sodium Thiopental, Abbott)

James C. Mc Larnan MD
104 E. Gambier St
Mount Vernon Ohio 43050
U.S.A.

New Zealand · Mt. Egmont and the pasture lands of Taranaki (1961)

186

NEW ZEALAND:
Mt. Egmont and the pasture lands of Taranaki

PRINTED MATTER

PENTOTHAL® (Thiopental, Abbott)

A

Dear Doctor:
From makers of the
PENTOTHAL family of
intravenous anesthetics,
Holiday Greetings! We've
chosen this New Zealand
stamp depicting Rembrandt's
"Adoration of the Shepherds"
as especially appropriate
to the Christmas season.
Abbott

DR. MARJORIE R. HOPPER,
278 N. MIDLAND AVE.,
NYACK, N. Y.
U. S. A.

Australia Antarctica Territory · Wilkes, Australian Antarctica (1961) · Charles Wilkes led the US Expedition, from 1838 – 1842.

WILKES, AUSTRALIAN ANTARCTIC.

188

Dear Doctor:

In the frigid expanse of
Antarctica, men from many
nations staff the geo-physical
stations, gathering scientific
data. Doctors here demand
-and get- the utmost in dependability and safety in their
medical supplies. One of these
is PENTOTHAL, agent of choice
the world over in intravenous
anesthesia.

Abbott

PENTOTHAL® [Thiopental Sodium, Abbott]

Selected Readings

About the cards:

Chicorz R: "Lundy Pentothal Postcards with Non-English Language Text." *Lundy Collectors Club Quarterly*, Summer, 1996.

Friedman D: "Advertising postcards: the story behind Pentathol sodium cards by Abbott." *Barr's Post Card News*, July 19, 1993, Issue #567.

Griffenhagen G: "Stamps Promoting Medicines." *International Pharmacy Journal* 1995; 9:1.

Griffenhagen G and Day JR: "Abbott Laboratories 'Round the World' Campaign." *Scalpel & Tongs* 1984; 28: 117-119.

Haeseler R: "'Dear Doctor' Card Club Forming." *Linn's Stamp News*, October 13, 2003.

Hotchner JM: "New collecting areas kindle new interests." *Linn's Stamp News*, November 13, 1995.

Krejci MG: "Recent Advertising Cover Discoveries." *Vatican Notes* 2003; 52:3:1,15-18.

Kyle RA, Shampo MA: "Medicine and Stamps." *AMA*, 1970.

Lai DC: "Around the World: an Introduction to Pentothal Advertising Postcards from Abbott Laboratories, 1956-1968." *HAS Proceedings 2002*; 31:29-31.

McKenzie AG: "A History of Anesthesia through Postage Stamps." Edinburgh, *Maclean Dubois*, 2000, pp 34-39.

Ratz H: "A Postmark Collector's Delight." *Liechtenstudy 2002*; October.

Slosman E: "The Portugese Pentothal Card." *American Philatelist* 2001; August: 726-727.

Walker M: "The Pentothal Advertising Postcards Posted from Wilkes Base." *Philately in Australia 2001*.

Selected medical references:

Bennetts FE: Thiopentone, Chicago to Pearl Harbor. AHA Newsletter 1992; 10:8-11.

Cope DK, Calmes SH and Stephen CR: AHA [Anesthesia History Association] Newsletters (1982-1995). Canton, MA, Watson Publishing International, 1996.

Dundee JW and Riding JE: Barbiturate narcosis in porphyria. Anaesthesia 1955; 10:55-58.

Hunter AR: Twenty years ago: Pentothal sodium anaesthesia. Anaesthesia 1968; 23:450-458.

Hyzler G: Speech by the acting President. Malta DOI No. 1040.

Lai DC: Barrell of Lunatics. Park Ridge, WLM, 2003.

Lai DC: Holding Court With the Ghost of Gilman Terrace. Park Ridge, WLM, 2002.

Waters, M.D. "Park Ridge, Wood Library-Museum of Anesthesiology, 2002.

Lundy JS: From this point in time: Some memories of my part in the history of anesthesia. AANA Journal 1966:24:95-102.

Pender JW: John S. Lundy, M.D.: AA Festschrift." AHA Newsletter 1987; 5:4, 1, 4-9, 16.

Pierce EC: "The 34th Rovenstine Lecture: 40 Years behind the Mask: Safety Revisited." Anesthesiology 1996; 84:965-975. Available at http://www.anesthesiology.org and http://www.apsf.org.

Pratt TW, Tatum AL, Hathaway HR and Waters RM: "Sodium Ethyl (1-methyl butyl) Thiobarbiturates." Am J Sung 1936; 31: 464-466.

Steinhaus JE. Ralph M. Waters, M.D. "A Teacher's Teacher." AHA Newsletter 1988; 6:2:1, 3-8.

Presented in part at the History of Anaesthesia Society 2002 Autumn Meeting, Sheffield, UK. Supported in part by grants from the Beth Israel Anesthesia Foundation, Boston, MA and Abbott Laboratories, Abbott Park, IL.

190

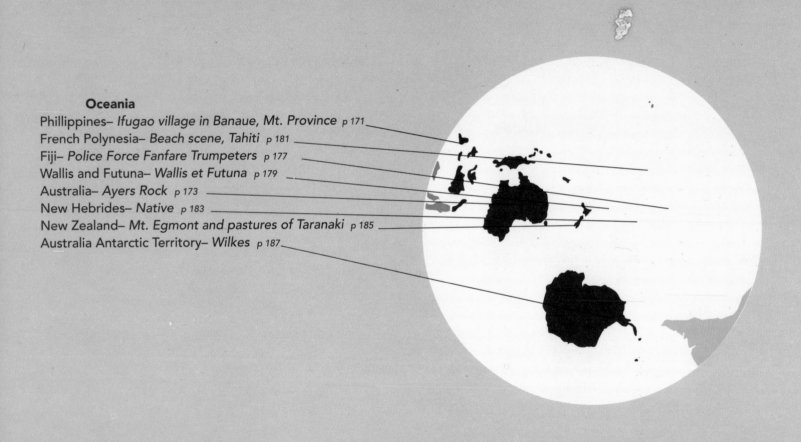